The Twelve Holy Nights

The Twelve Holy Nights

Meditations on The Dream Song of Olaf Åsteson

Commentary by Frans Lutters

Illustrated by Hans-Dieter Appenrodt

Floris Books

Introduction and Commentary translated by Philip Mees
The Dream Song of Olaf Åsteson translated by Eleanor Merry

First published in Dutch as
De 12 Heilige Nachten: Het Droomlied van Olaf Åsteson
by Christofoor Publishers, Zeist in 2013
First published in English by Floris Books in 2018
Second printing 2022

British Library CIP Data available
ISBN 978-178250-528-0

Contents

Origin and Significance of the Dream Song

Bernard Lievegoed

In about 1850, in a lonely valley in Telemark in southern Norway, Magnus Landstad (1802–80) wrote down the *Dream Song of Olaf Åsteson* as he heard it out of the mouths of the local story-tellers. The song was in the Old Norwegian language and became an element in the language struggle of Norway, in which Old Norwegian won out over Urban Norwegian in the end, which was actually Danish.

During a visit to Oslo in 1919, Rudolf Steiner's attention was drawn to the *Dream Song* by the Norwegian author Ingeborg Möller-Lindholm. At his request, she made a word-for-word translation which he later worked on himself. Since then, Rudolf Steiner spoke more than once about the *Dream Song* and on these occasions Marie Steiner recited the text in German. Rudolf Steiner's lectures have shown the importance of this old saga also for our time.

The *Dream Song of Olaf Åsteson* is only a fragment of a much greater whole, but what is special is that it has preserved all the elements of the Norse path of initiation.

Who was Olaf Åsteson? To find a historical connection we have to go back to the time around the year 1000, when the then Germanic-pagan land of Norway was touched by Christianity through two great kings, Olaf I and Olaf II. Olaf I, Tryggvason, lived from about 960 to 1000. He came from Estonia as a slave, spent his youth in Novgorod, Russia, and later sailed as a Viking to France and England.

Through a hermit on the Scilly Isles he became Celtic Christian, and later he married the Christian daughter of an Irish king. Back in Norway he became king in 995 and began the conversion of the country to Christianity. He also wanted to conquer Sweden, but he was killed in 1000 during a naval battle in his ship *Great Serpent,* the largest vessel of its day. Olaf Tryggvason was the archetypal image of the Viking king and initiate, with all the courage and wildness of the Norse path of initiation. For him, who had had an encounter with the 'Great Guardian,' the transition to Celtic cosmic Christianity was a natural step.

Olaf II, Haraldson, was born in 995, the year when Olaf I became king. He had already met Christianity in his youth but, as is apparent from the Song, had also gone through a northern path of initiation which did not clash with western Celtic Christianity. He also went as a Viking to England when still very young and returned in 1015 as a twenty-year-old. In 1016 he fought the ruler of the time in a battle and became king of Norway. The Christianisation of Norway was then carried through with great force, which generated much opposition. In 1029 there was a revolt of the nobility led by Knut the Great. Olaf fled to Russia, returned in 1030 and fell in the battle of Stiklestad fighting his own Norwegians. His cruelty and violence were forgotten. His tomb became a place of pilgrimage where miracles of healing occurred. In 1164 he was canonised and he is revered as Saint Olaf to this day.

Olaf Haraldson's mother had the name Åste. The name has two meanings, first, 'love' and, second, 'the blood stream in which clairvoyance still lives.' Through his mother, therefore, Olaf Åsteson had a hereditary connection with the old mysteries of courage, while through his environment he came into contact with a cosmic Christianity, in which, following Celtic tradition, Christ was experienced as the king of the elements. In his soul lived the duality that is characteristic for a time of transition, and his biography must not be judged with common criteria.

In addition to the historical aspect, however, there is, as always in this kind of subject, a spiritual background that shines through the history. Rudolf Steiner has pointed out that the name Olaf Åsteson, as also the name of King Arthur, can be viewed as a mystery name borne by multiple generations, and also that the *content* of the Song has an earlier origin than the *form* in which it was handed down; the form dates back to the thirteenth century. He spoke about this with Ingeborg Möller who made notes of his remarks. One passage from these notes reads:

The content of the *Dream Song* is supposed to be much older than is generally assumed, and dates from about AD 400. There was at that time a great Christian initiate in Norway, whose mystery name was Olaf Åsteson, and the song describes his initiation. He founded a mystery school in the southern area of the country; the name of the place was not mentioned. The song was originally much longer and had twelve parts, one for every sign of the zodiac. That song described Olaf Åsteson's journey through the world of stars and what he saw and experienced there. The current version comprises only the remnants of the original song. The mystery school referred to above was still in existence in the early Middle Ages, and the leader was always called Olaf Åsteson.

These remarks by the spiritual investigator also throw light on Saint Olaf. Perhaps this king was also in this sense an Olaf Åsteson. Essentially the *Dream Song* reflects a path of initiation.

In the *Dream Song* as we now know it, Olaf is pictured as an initiate who goes through a mystery sleep in the twelve Holy Nights between Christmas and Epiphany. He can relate his experiences to the churchgoers on January 6. His song contains all the elements of the Norse cosmic path of initiation, but in a later time period, so that the pictures are mixed with Christian elements.

The stages on the path are marked by the changes in the refrain. After an introduction, the etheric world is spoken of: 'The Moon shone bright, and the paths were far to follow.' This is the passage through the elemental world, through heights of clouds; he is thrown into turbid mires, crosses divine streams, moves through thorny moors, and sees masses of ice as blue flames.

Then he comes to the Gjaller Bridge, which leads to another area. The bridge is guarded by three beasts: a hound, a serpent and a bull, a kind of 'Norse sphinx' – spirit serpent, spirit hound and spirit bull. Only those who honour truth may pass the bridge.

Again the path goes through bogs, through earth and through ice. He chooses the winter path, the Milky Way, and from afar the light of Paradise is already shining. Then he sees God's Holy Mother who points him to purgatory, kamaloka, here called Brokksvalin. The refrain then changes: 'In Brokksvalin shall the judgement be.' It is the realm where souls undergo the world of judgement. Olaf then experiences all the consequences of earthly guilt. It is clearly an astral realm: from the north evil spirits come riding in, led by the Prince of Hell himself. But from the south comes Saint Michael at the side of Jesus Christ. Christ is here the world judge, the Greater Guardian, who watches how Michael weighs the souls.

Then comes the final part, the sanctification. The refrain is then: 'The tongue shall speak and truth attest on Judgement Day.' The 'tongue' of Michael's scales speaks, and wisdom sounds in spiritual being. This part creates the impression that it is of a later time; it lacks the stricter form of the previous parts.

Where the translation has the phrase 'God's Holy Mother', the Norwegian has *gudmor,* godmother, but this can also be interpreted as God's Mother.

The figure of *Grutte Grå-skjegge* (grim Grey-beard) was called the Prince of Hell or Ahriman by Ingeborg Möller.

When he travelled through a 'thorny moorland', Olaf's scarlet mantle was torn: 'My scarlet mantle was torn awry'. The scarlet mantle indicates that Olaf was of royal blood. He was that also in the world across the threshold, meaning that he was fully initiated.

Working with the Holy Nights

Frans Lutters

In our time, many people are searching for spiritual deepening in their lives. This is especially true for the time of the Holy Nights between Christmas and Epiphany. This particular time of the year may be rediscovered in a new way. In this brief contribution I will describe possible ways that may lead to a more profound experience of the time of the Holy Nights. Out of more than thirty years' experience, and by holding workshops in many different places, a method has evolved that works well from many different points of view.

During a dark winter, between Christmas and Epiphany long, long ago, Olaf Åsteson had an extraordinary experience which can be viewed as an initiation into the great secrets of existence. After this experience, Olaf had become spiritually stronger and felt better prepared for his responsibilities. The same is true for each one of us. Our lives today place great demands on us requiring vision and decisiveness. Working in a special way with the Holy Nights can give us an inspiring potential to step into the New Year with greater consciousness and enthusiasm.

The Dream Song
of Olaf Åsteson

Come listen to me and hear my song
The song of a wondrous youth,
 I'll sing of Olaf Åsteson
 Who slept many days – 'tis the truth.
  Yes, it was Olaf Åsteson
  Who lay so long a-sleeping.

It was Christmas Eve when down he lay
And slept so long all unknowing,
 He never woke till the thirteenth day
 When to Church the people were going.
  Yes, it was Olaf Åsteson
  Who lay so long a-sleeping.

'Twas the Holy Night when down he lay
Such wonders seeing and hearing
     And wakened not till the thirteenth day
     When the drowsy birds were stirring.
          Yes, it was Olaf Åsteson
          Who lay so long a-sleeping.

He never woke till the thirteenth day
When the Sun came up at dawning,
     Then he saddled his horse and rode away
     To ride to Church in the morning.
          Yes, it was Olaf Åsteson
          Who lay so long a-sleeping.

The Priest he stood at the altar there
The Holy Gospel expounding,
     While Olaf sat down at the outer door
     And told of his visions astounding.
          Yes, it was Olaf Åsteson
          Who lay so long a-sleeping.

The Holy Nights

The Twelve Holy Nights begin on Christmas Eve and end in the morning of Epiphany on January 6. They consist of twelve nights. The first night, Christmas night, is actually separate; the twelve nights follow after that night. The Holy Nights as a whole, strictly speaking, encompass thirteen nights, 1 and 12 is 13.

The time between Christmas and Epiphany has always been known as a time in which people can better remember their dreams. It seems as if in this time of year we can better live into our dreams and can also explain them. In ancient times, in the northern countries of Europe, this time was sometimes called the time 'between the years.' And in a certain sense it was a time 'between the years.'

A month was then seen as being 29½ days long, the period from new moon to new moon. Today this period is called the synodic month or lunar month. Twelve times 29½ days equals 354 days, leaving 11 days – twelve nights – before the solar year of about 365 days is completed. There was a kind of lacuna in the calendar, and this time had originally no dates.

These twelve nights after Christmas were therefore not time, but space. In an old rune calendar the time is indicated as the moment 'between the years,' leaving room for encounters, companionship, sleep and now and then a sizeable beaker of honey mead. It was in such a period that Olaf Åsteson made his long dream journey lasting for twelve nights. He fell asleep the night after Christmas.

Christmas night itself is a night that calls for special awareness. To this day farm families in Scandinavia make the rounds of their stables to sing to the animals on Christmas night.

A practical exercise

In our day the time between Christmas and Epiphany is still experienced as a special time of the year. Many people feel the need to visit each other and do nice things with the family. They go to a concert, or a show; they take a walk in the Christmas mood of the countryside, and do many other pleasant things. But there is also frequently a longing for inner deepening and meditative moments. Music, a story, or a good conversation may then feel just right. In recent decades something new seems to be growing around efforts to work concretely with the Holy Nights in a fully contemporary manner.

The aged men and the younger ones too –
His tale for a past-time taking –
    Hear Olaf Åsteson tell them true
    His Dream-filled sleep and awakening.
        Yes, it was Olaf Åsteson
        Who lay so long a-sleeping.

I laid me down on this Christmas night,
In sleep profound and unending,
    And wakened not till the thirteenth day
    When all to the Church were wending.
        The Moon shone bright
        And the paths were far to follow.

I wandered far, above the cloudy wrack,
In depths of the ocean after –
    But he who travels along my track
    On his lips there will never be laughter.
        The Moon shone bright
        And the paths were far to follow.

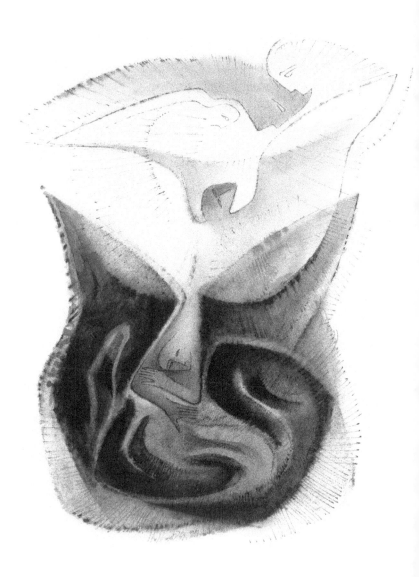

I wandered above in cloudy height
And plunged in bottomless waters,
   And depths of Hell have burned in my sight,
   I've glimpsed the heavenly pastures.
      The Moon shone bright
      And the paths were far to follow.

And I have forded the holy stream
And through the deep valleys going
   I heard the waters and saw them not –
   Beneath the Earth they were flowing.
      The Moon shone bright
      And the paths were far to follow.

Never a whinny came from my horse
Never a cry from my houndling,
   Nor any note of a singing bird
   Such wonders there were abounding.
      The Moon shone bright
      And the paths were far to follow.

Increasingly people use the time between Christmas and Epiphany for reflection, bringing things to consciousness. Groups have formed in the course of time of people who support each other for the preparation and actively work with the time of the Holy Nights. I had the good fortune to assist at many of such gatherings. Year after year a fruitful way of working grew to take advantage of this time 'between the years' in an agile yet earnest manner. Out of this work I would like to suggest a number of ways to make the time of the Holy Nights an inspiring and creative experience.

The day and night book

First of all, you can decide to pay attention to your dreams every night. Just like Olaf Åsteson you will notice that this resolution alone already has an influence on the quality of your dreams and the clarity with which they stay with you after you wake up. You can strengthen this resolution by using a notebook or sketchbook so as not to forget the dreams. For the frustration with dreams is that they fade so quickly if we do nothing with them. Thus, once we have made this preparation, a notebook or sketchbook is waiting for us by our bedside at Christmas Eve.

At first my sense was ravished away,
I fled through the thorny moorland,
My scarlet mantle was torn away,
The nails of my feet were wounded.
The Moon shone bright
And the paths were far to follow.

Oh then I came to the Gjaller Bridge
So high in the winds suspended,
And all with gold were its beams bedecked
And spikes with its rafters blended.
The Moon shone bright
And the paths were far to follow.

The serpent strikes, and savage the hound,
In the middle lies the traverse,
Three dread things on the Gjaller mound –
And all are crooked and monstrous.
The Moon shone bright
And the paths were far to follow.

The serpent strikes and the fierce hound bites,
The bull stands ready to ram me –
    None will pass over the Gjaller heights
    Who with judgement false have damned.
        The Moon shone bright
        And the paths were far to follow.

But I have crossed over the Gjaller Bridge
Stern passage so grim and olden,
    Have waded through mournful swamps and sedge
    And now I am free and unholden.
        The Moon shone bright
        And the paths were far to follow.

Waded have I through mire of despair
My pathways were never on Earth,
    And thus did I climb the Gjaller stair
    With the dust of death in my mouth.
        The Moon shone bright
        And the paths were far to follow.

And then I came where the waters part
From fiery blue to burning ice,
    But God did put it into my heart
    To pass, and turn away mine eyes.
        The Moon shone bright
        And the paths were far to follow.

I went my way by the winter road
Which turned aside at my right hand,
    Faint glimpses of Paradise it showed
    And a light lay over the land.
        The Moon shone bright
        And the paths were far to follow.

God's Holy Mother did I see there –
O nothing better could befall! –
    "Now go on thy way to Brokksvalin
    Thy way unto the Judgement Hall."
        In Brokksvalin
        Shall the Judgement be.

Christmas Eve

Then the time has come. In the evening of December 24 open the notebook. And now follows an important decision. For in this evening of the birth of the Christ Child you write on the first page the subject you want to work with this year during the Holy Nights. You have endless possibilities for this theme, and therefore it is good to start contemplating some of these already during Advent, the time of preparation for Christmas. The idea is that you stay with the same theme throughout the whole period of the Holy Nights.

Thus the twelve nights following Christmas Eve are dedicated to a self-chosen theme. Again, there are many themes. In the course of the years many subjects have been chosen, such as twelve composers. The person who chose this was a musician himself and played something each night, but we might also just listen, alone or with others.

We might also look back on the past twelve months and talk, write or make drawings about them. The sequence is free and is best left to one's own intuition, but it is a good idea to determine the sequence in advance, on Christmas Eve at the latest. We do this by writing each successive date on two facing pages in the notebook, from December 24 to January 5, keeping the last two pages for January 6, the day when

There was I in that other world
Through many nights and long,
    And God in Heaven knoweth well
    What fearful things among.
        In Brokksvalin
        Shall the Judgement be.

And there I met a wicked man
The first that I did see –
    A little boy was in his arms
    He waded to the knee.
        In Courts of Pain
        Shall the Judgement be.

And when I came up close to him.
His mantle was of lead,
    For in this world his soul was bound
    In bitter bonds of greed.
        In Courts of Pain
        Shall the Judgement be.

the Holy Nights come to an end. A notebook with one page for writing and one for drawing is of course also a possibility.

Another theme may be related to the twelve signs of the zodiac, including perhaps people you know who were born under a certain sign. What is nice about this alternative is that it consists of twelve signs so that every night one of them can get your attention. The point is not to be complete, or make an exhaustive study. It is quite sufficient to read something together or contemplate a work of art on the subject of the theme, and to write or draw something yourself. And if you get a visitor or the children are at home, just let them take part in it. Most of all, keep an inspiring and comfortable atmosphere.

Another subject is perhaps more conducive to drawing, if we love crystals and perhaps have a number of them in the house, such as amethyst, pyrite, or others. And there may even be a book in which we can read something about each crystal in the evening.

Other subjects may be different trees that play, or have played, a role in your life, or twelve persons who are important to you, such as artists, authors or scientists. Even twelve languages or twelve paintings may form a theme.

Evening work

Every night we write or draw something about the chosen theme that occurred to us or came up in conversation. Here too, the sequence is free as long as you have set a sequence in the notebook before the beginning of the Twelve Nights.

If we consistently do something concrete with the notebook or sketchbook every evening, we create an opening for very special experiences. Why is this work in the evening so important? Many years' experience show that this activity is comparable to putting a stamp on the envelope of a letter. But now, this letter is going to a very particular part of our world, namely the world where we sojourn every night, especially during the Holy Nights. The subject we work with those twelve nights acts like a focal point on our experiences in the night, and brings, when we wake up, significant ideas and dreams.

Morning mail

Many people who have worked for years in this way have found that it seems as if they receive an answer in the morning in the form of a dream, a thought or an experience. The dream, thought or experience has no ostensible connection with the subject we are working with. But the activity of the evening makes

And many men drew near to me –
Each carried burning sod,
    May God have pity on their souls,
    They'd moved the landmarks in the wood.
        In affliction's courts
        Shall the Judgement be.

Children came up along the ways
Walking on coals of fire –
    May God have mercy on their souls
    Who cursed their parents dear,
        In Courts of Pain
        Shall the Judgement be.

To the House of Shame I made my way
Where witches together crowded,
    I saw them standing in crimson blood
    With such evil were they loaded.
        In Brokksvalin
        Shall the Judgement be.

us more awake and actively engaged with what we wake up to. It is as if we receive return mail. Then it becomes important to do something with this return mail. Again, talk about it with someone, write or draw something, or write it down just like a story. A good place to do this is on the reverse of the page you used the previous evening, or simply on a new page marked with the date and morning. You can do more on that page, such as make a poem or write or draw something about the weather, the news, nature, or perhaps a visit. It need not be long; all you need are little activities to make the process work.

Obstacles

This is a good place to take a look at the obstacles that we may run into on our journey through the Holy Nights.

The first obstacle is that you cannot find a theme. You might ask someone else, or take a good look over your bookshelves, garden or calendar to find a subject that can be divided into twelve.

Another obstacle may be that you don't work in your notebook for days and have totally forgotten about it. You may think that the project has failed and you just let it be. Why? You can catch up, but first continue with the date where you remembered the work. On the empty pages you can look back on the past days.

Such heat there burns in the depths of Hell!
A heat no man can imagine.
> They bended over their cauldron well
> And flung a sinner's body in.
>> In Brokksvalin
>> Shall the Judgement be.

The hunt came faring out of the North
Riding along so quick and crack –
> And right in the front rode grim Grey-beard
> Leading his hell-wild hunting pack.
>> In Brokksvalin
>> Shall the Judgement be.

The hunt came faring out of the North
The blackest hunt methinks of all
> And right in the front rode grim Grey-beard
> On a stallion black as a pall.
>> In Brokksvalin
>> Shall the Judgement be.

Then came the faring out of the South
And all that came were quiet and blest,
    For now in the front St Michael rode
    And at his side was Jesus Christ.
        In Brokksvalin
        Shall the Judgement be.

From southwards they came, and more and more
Most noble was the pageant now –
    'Twas Michael of Souls rode on before
    And his horse was whiter than snow.
        In Brokksvalin
        Shall the Judgement be.

Out of the South came riding the host
It seemed in never-ending bands,
    The Holy Michael of Souls foremost,
    Who carried healing in his hands.
        In Brokksvalin
        Shall the Judgement be.

As a last resort you can always put in the Christmas cards you received or ask children or friends to write or draw something in your notebook. Working on the theme and the notebook does not need to be a mysterious, lonely activity at all. Just let others help you if you can't make a go of it yourself.

If you have no dreams, experiences or thoughts when you wake up in the morning, or if anything lingers from the night that is absurd, just keep at it. Experience shows that there will be at least one special dream, sometimes not until the last day.

If you have a lot of visitors or a lot of work, make it interesting for the visitors to participate, or ask others in the morning about their dreams or experiences.

Then there is another obstacle that often occurs in the course of the process. During the time to New Year's Eve things are going all right, but then you suddenly lose steam. The period between Christmas and New Year's Eve is usually a nice time because of the long, cosy winter evenings. All the houses have Christmas trees, there are Christmas concerts, and so on. But after New Year everything returns to normal. The sun sets a few minutes later in the afternoon already. Now is the time to persevere. The period between New Year and Epiphany is important. Try to last through the twelve nights, otherwise there are only seven, and that is not enough.

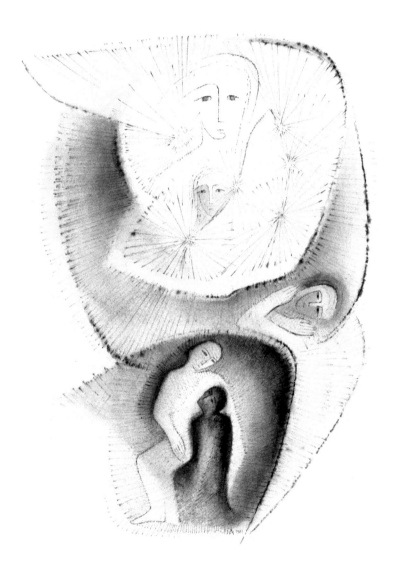

Michael the Lord of Souls it was then
Who blew long and loud on his horn,
    Calling to all the souls to go in
    To the Judgement so dread and lorn.
        In Courts of Pain
        Shall the Judgement be.

See how the sinful souls are a-shake
Like the aspen leaves blown by the wind,
    And never a single soul is there
    But weeping knows well it has sinned.
        In affliction's courts
        Shall the Judgement be.

It was St Michael, holy and good
Who ever in his balance cast
    The trembling souls that around his stood
    And bore them to Jesus at last.
        In Brokksvalin
        Shall the Judgement be.

It may help to change the theme a little after the New Year. You can do this, for instance, by choosing seven artists for the time between Christmas and New Year's Eve, and five scientists for the evenings to Epiphany. Christmas is connected with the shepherds. Countless artists have honoured the Child in the manger with their artworks, while after New Year the scientists as the Wise Men bring their insights as gifts. The period until New Year's Eve is more a time of the warmth of heart of the shepherds, whereas the time after New Year is connected with the clear thinking of the Three Wise Men. When we prepare for the Holy Nights out of the dynamic of shepherds and kings, of heart and head, you will find that working with the Holy Nights is easier to sustain.

Rounding off

We round off the Holy Nights on January 6, which is also the morning when long ago Olaf Åsteson awoke and rode to the church to relate his dreams. For the work with the Holy Nights we round off our notebook or sketchbook on this day, at least for the time being. Once more we can look through all we have written or drawn and perhaps write down a new thought or fill a gap here or there. Then we conclude our work.

Blessed is he who here on Earth
Gives shoes unto the poor,
For he may walk the thorny heath
With naked feet and sure.
The tongue shall speak
And truth attest on Judgement Day.

Blessed is he who in this world
Gives bread unto the poor
He has no fear in spirit-land
When hungry hounds draw near.
The tongue shall speak
And truth attest on Judgement Day.

Blessed is he who here on Earth
Shall give the poor his corn,
He will not fear on Gjaller Bridge
The Bull's sharp-thrusting horn.
The tongue shall speak
And truth attest on Judgement Day.

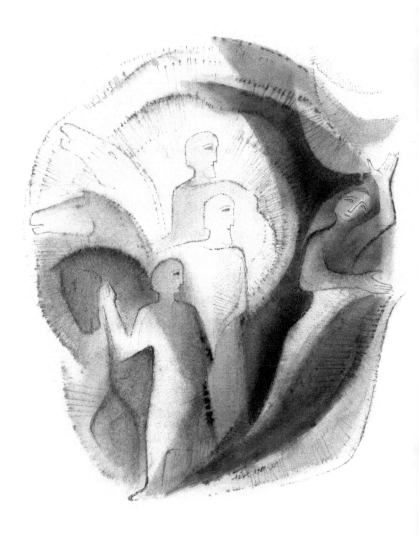

Blessed is he who here on Earth
His clothes the naked brings,
    He need not fear in the other world
    The dreadful frozen springs.
        The tongue shall speak
        And truth attest on Judgement Day.

The aged man and young men too
Have listened and attended
    To his, to Olaf Åsteson
    Whose Dream-song now is ended.
        Rise up, thou Olaf Åsteson
        Thou hast been so long-a-sleeping!

Perhaps we have a card we want to paste in, or we want to change something on the outside of the book to reflect what it has in the meantime become.

The journey through the Holy Nights has come to an end this year. The notebook can be put away. But it may happen that it takes you another couple of weeks, or perhaps even to Easter, to really understand certain experiences. If that happens, don't hesitate to go back to the book. It can be your accompanying friend for the whole year.

You will notice that working with the Holy Nights will become a new longing you can look forward to when Christmas is approaching again. Next year you will feel like choosing a theme again and put the mail in the form of dreams, ideas and encounters into a new notebook or sketchbook.

Here is my warning: this is special work, it brings joy and becomes part of your life. The Holy Nights come to life and become a new tradition for a special time of the year.

I wish you much enjoyment and inspiration on this extraordinary journey through the Holy Nights. Olaf Åsteson travelled this road as a king's son a thousand years ago in Scandinavia; we can follow a similar one in a new way when we set out with an open mind and our notebook or sketchbook.

About the Original Norwegian

Frans Lutters

It is perhaps not quite correct to speak of *the* Dream Song of Olaf Åsteson, for in the course of the past century and a half several versions and translations have been published. The one in this book is one of those.

The original edition of the *Norske Folkeviser* (Christiania 1853) of the pastor-poet and folk-song collector Magnus Brostrup Landstad contains two versions of the *Draumkvedet,* the *Dream Song.* The first is a short one, 30 stanzas, the way he wrote it down from the mouth of Maren Ramskeid of Kviteseid in Telemark; it seems to be a rendition as she remembered it piece by piece, which is the reason that it is rather fragmentary. The second and later version, in which some earlier stanzas were left out and the *Dream Song* was increased to 60 stanzas found elsewhere, has a clearer storyline.

In the second half of the nineteenth century, the *Dream Song* played an important role in Norway's struggle for independence. In 1894 an edition of

54 stanzas appeared, created by the folklorist and linguist Ingebret Moltke Moe, and in 1901 the Norwegian singer Thorvald Lammers published a shortened version of this with 40 stanzas that he had in his singing repertory. This is probably the version Ingeborg Möller-Lindholm used for the literal translation from which Rudolf Steiner later created his rendition of 36 stanzas.

An edition from 1927 by Ivar Mortensen-Egnund is a compilation of 119 stanzas including material from other ballads from Landstad's *Folkeviser*. Here the hero's journey along the signs of the zodiac – which has been suggested by some commentators – is reconstructed, but in other respects it has little to do with the *Dream Song* of Landstad.

As to the form of the *Dream Song,* every line has a fixed number of stressed syllables and around these – before, between, after, and sometimes not at all – there are an indeterminate, but not unlimited, number of unaccented syllables. Thus it is a rhythmical, not metric form of verse.

The structure of the stanzas has a striking similarity of form with the Old-Norse *Ljothahattr* (song measure) that was used for 'mystical' verse, such as mantras, aphorisms and the like, that occur, for instance, in *Hávemál* (Songs of the High One) of the *Edda*. They have twice one line with four stressed syllables plus one line with three, held together by alliteration. However, the refrains have a different form.

Here and there we can find traces of alliteration, but it is not a notable characteristic of this older folk ballad. What is characteristic are the many repetitions and terse expressions we are also familiar with from other countries' medieval literature.

Eleanor Merry's translation in this book has 40 stanzas and is probably translated from the version Ingeborg Möller-Lindholm used.

For news on all our **latest books,**
and to receive **exclusive discounts,**
join our mailing list at:

florisbooks.co.uk

Plus subscribers get a FREE book
with every online order!

We will never pass your details to anyone else.